ONE YEAR WISER

THE COLORING BOOK

First published 2016
by SelfMadeHero
139-141 Pancras Road
London NW1 1UN
www.selfmadehero.com

Images copyright © 2015 Mike Medaglia

Illustrated by Mike Medaglia

Publishing Assistant: Guillaume Rater
Sales & Marketing Manager: Sam Humphrey
US Publicist: Maya Bradford
Publishing Director: Emma Hayley
Designer: Kate McLauchlan

A CIP record for this book is available from the British Library

ISBN: 978-1-910593-14-1

10 9 8 7 6 5 4 3 2 1

Printed and bound in Slovenia

ONE YEAR WISER

THE COLORING BOOK

Unwind with
Weekly Illustrated Meditations

MIKE MEDAGLIA

SELF MADE HERO

Introduction

On their own, words and pictures can be a source of great change – both personally and for the world as a whole. But when brought together, they create a unique and powerful combination. With *One Year Wiser*, I wanted to create images that enhance the words of the great thinkers and doers quoted in this book, presenting their wisdom in a new way. The final element of this coloring book is left up to you: to add color to these pages and bring the ideas fully to life!

As an artist, my work reflects the world I'm living in, which is too often filled with cynicism, so I try to focus on hope and positivity. I created the images for this book as intuitively as possible, letting them manifest out of the words themselves. I have often found encouragement and comfort in aphorisms and inspirational quotes from wise and witty people. A well-crafted quotation can distill an idea, capturing its impact. This same approach can be applied to coloring. When you sit down to draw, take a deep breath. Focus on the image and the words and just color the pages using whatever colors feel right. Take the time to relax. Unwind. Have fun! Experiment with different mediums and colors. You can use pencil crayons for a soft, blended look or markers for boldness – or even your old crayons for youthful exuberance. Use this as an opportunity to focus on the wonderful act of creation.

These pages were all drawn by hand. I use pencil to draw the images and then ink them using a Japanese brush pen. The quotes I chose all came from people who have inspired me and my work. I hope they in turn will now inspire you!

Mike Medaglia

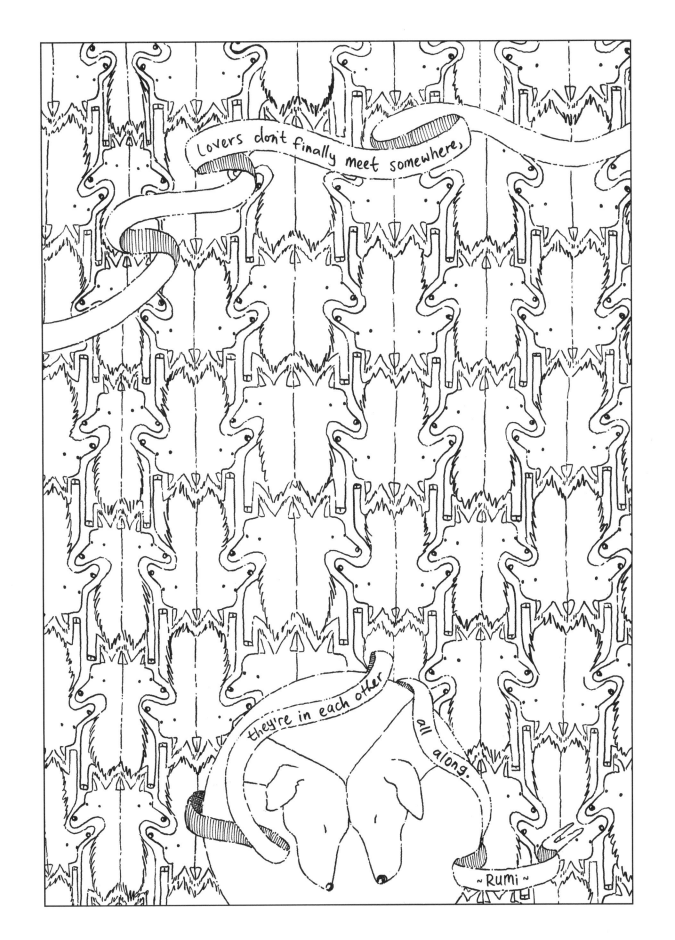

If you hear a voice within you say you cannot paint, then by all means paint and that voice will be silenced.

Vincent van Gogh

Yoga is the journey of the self

through the self

to the Self.

~The Bhagavad Gita~

INTELLIGENCE IS THE ABILITY TO ADAPT TO CHANGE

STEPHEN HAWKING

Generosity is the essence of friendship.

OSCAR WILDE

There is no passion to be found in playing small – in settling for a life that is less than the one you are capable of living.

NELSON MANDELA

BECAUSE EACH EXISTENCE IS IN CONSTANT CHANGE, THERE IS NO ABIDING SELF.

SHUNRYU SUZUKI

The POETRY of EARTH is NEVER dead

~John Keats~

Enlightenment
is the mind
which sees
into
impermanence.

DOGEN

AND THE DAY CAME WHEN THE RISK TO REMAIN

tight in
a bud was
more painful
than the risk
it took to
blossom.

ANAÏS NIN

TO BE ALIVE IN THIS BEAUTIFUL, SELF-ORGANIZING UNIVERSE --
TO PARTICIPATE IN THE DANCE OF LIFE WITH SENSES TO PERCEIVE
IT, LUNGS TO BREATHE IT, ORGANS THAT DRAW NOURISHMENT
FROM IT -- IS A WONDER BEYOND WORDS.

JOANNA MACY

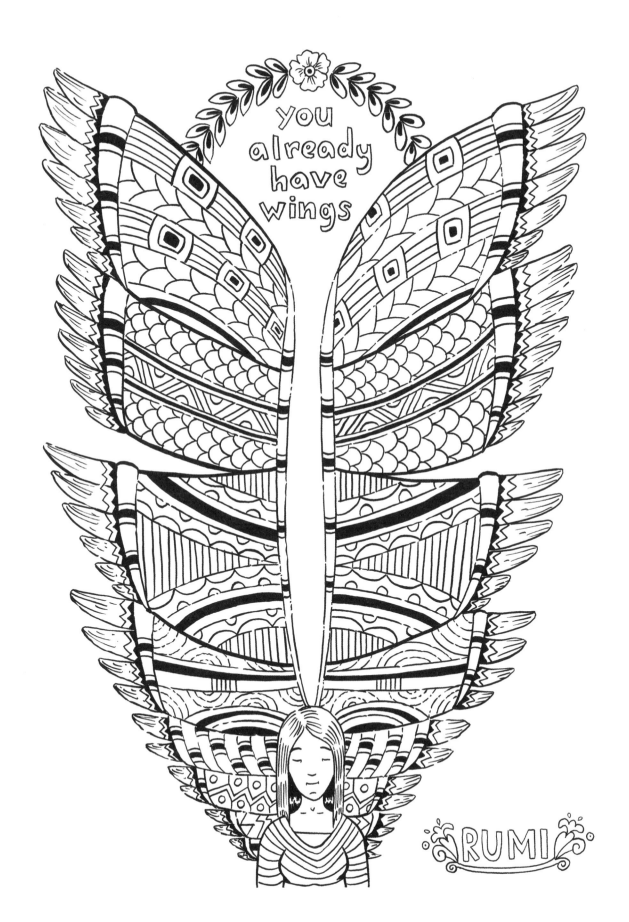

All dreams spin out from the same web.

NATIVE AMERICAN PROVERB

I think there are things for all of us to do as long as we're here and we're healthy.

~ GWENDOLYN BROOKS ~

Many people will walk in and out of your life,

but only true friends will leave footprints in your heart.

ELEANOR ROOSEVELT

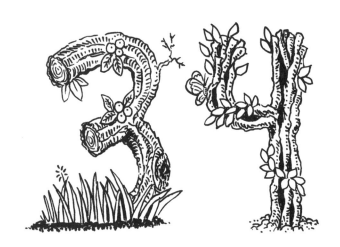

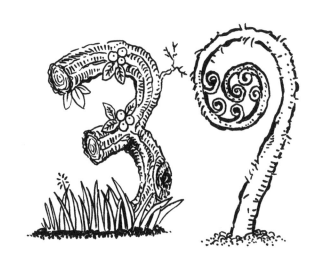

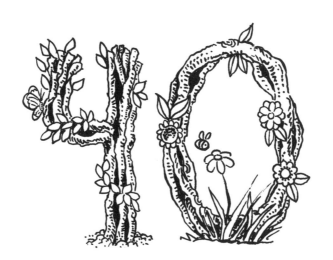

PERHAPS WE CANNOT RAISE THE WINDS. BUT EACH OF US CAN PUT UP THE SAIL, SO THAT WHEN THE WIND COMES WE CAN CATCH IT.
◦▥▥ E.F. SCHUMACHER ▥▥◦

If you take a flower in your hand and really look at it, it's your world for the moment.

GEORGIA O'KEEFFE

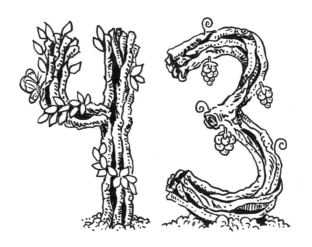

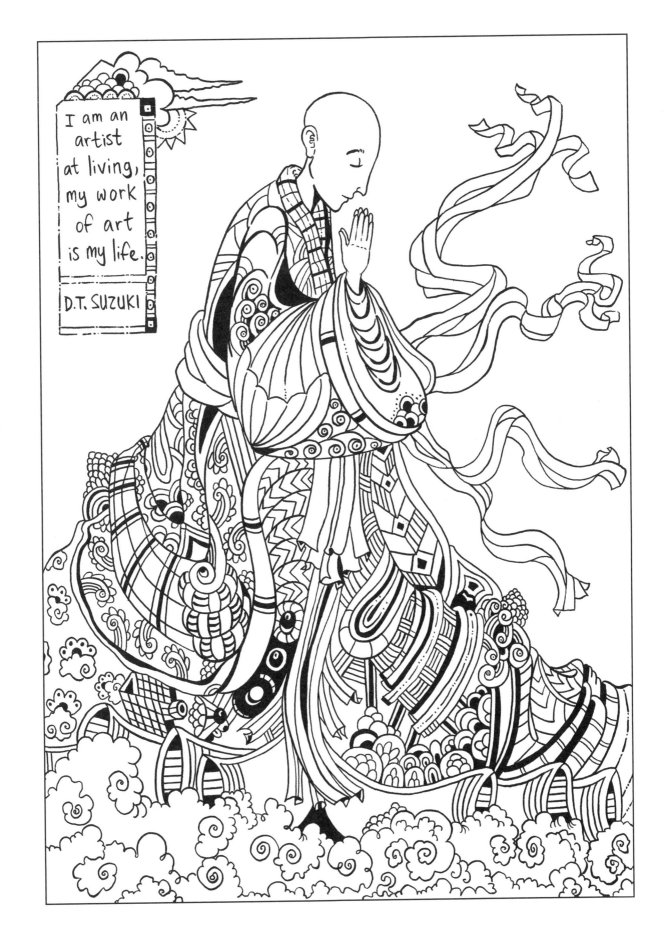

I am an
artist
at living,
my work
of art
is my life.

D.T. SUZUKI

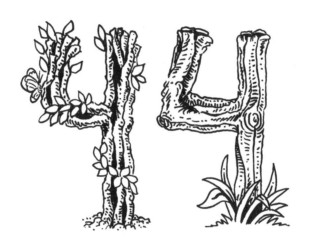

Be faithful
in small things
because it is in
them that
your strength lies.

MOTHER TERESA

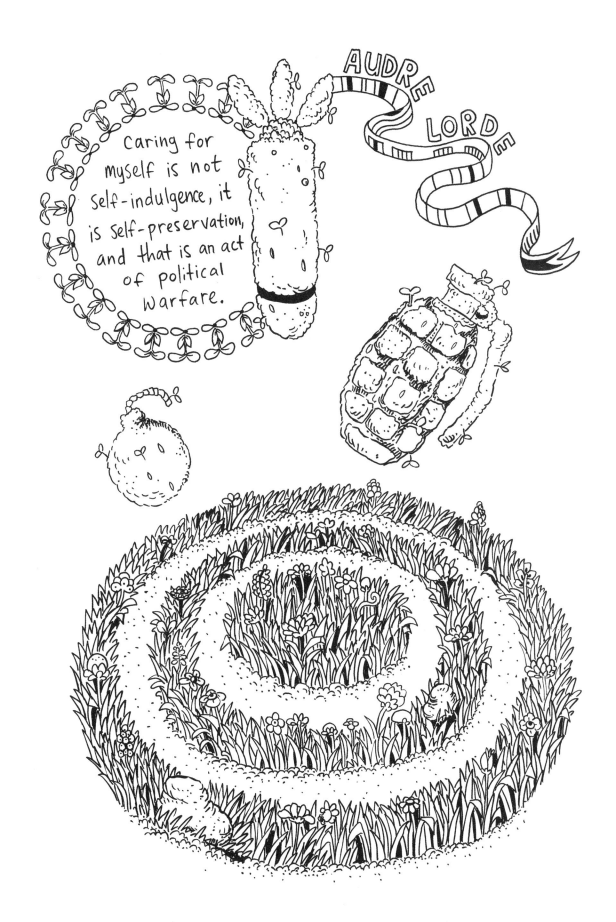

If we did all the things we are capable of doing, we would

LITERALLY ASTOUND OURSELVES

THOMAS A. EDISON

PALETTE

Use this area to try out your coloring utensils and get a feel for how they look

DOODLES

Have a go at filling this page with your own colorful drawings

QUOTES

Keep track of other inspirational quotes by writing them out here